HATHSU   SALES   F6316/POS1
SATURDAY 3 FEBRUARY 2018   11:31 086285
        SERT AID 2004124627 6316
1   OTHER BOOKS   £1.99
     2 x 11.9
2   OTHER BOOKS   £3.98

                        3 Items
     TOTAL   £5.97
     £20   £20.00
     CHANGE   £14.03
        Oxfam Shop F6316
        30, Brook Street,
  Broughty Ferry, Dundee, DD5 2AH
        01382 730237
        oxfam.org.uk/shop

WARM FUZZY GLOW – TO GO

Every item you buy or donate helps lift lives worldwide. Just £6 raised could train a health volunteer, helping communities in Bangladesh prepare for disaster.

www.oxfam.org.uk

LIFT
LIVES
FOR
GOOD

OXFAM

TAKE HOME SOME NECTAR POINTS

Donate your unwanted items to Oxfam and you can collect Nectar points when they're sold. Find out more at:

www.oxfam.org.uk/nectar

LIFT
LIVES

For the Sheer Hell of Living

Michael Glover was born in Sheffield, Yorkshire.
He has published five previous collections of poetry:

Measured Lives	(Dagger Press, 1994)
Impossible Horizons	(Sinclair-Stevenson, 1995)
A Small Modicum of Folly	(Dagger Press, 1997)
The Bead-Eyed Man	(Dagger Press, 1999)
Amidst all this Debris	(Dagger Press, 2001)

*with love to Jacqui
from Mich
15 Feby 2008*

FOR THE SHEER HELL OF LIVING

Michael Glover

San Marco Press
2008

First published 2008 by
San Marco Press
10 Lindum Road
Teddington
Middlesex
TW11 9DR

ISBN 978-0-9553739-7-8

Printed by Grafiche Nardin
Cavallino Treporti
Venezia

Grateful acknowledgement is made to the various publications in which some of these poems were first published: Thumbscrew, Stand, The London Magazine, Leviathan and P.N.R.

for Ruth, Joseph and Jesse

CONTENTS

For the sheer hell of living

Constable had a game he called Hope.
Every day he would throw the dice.
Every day he would watch them rolling.
This was before he conceived the notion
Of becoming a painter of landscapes.

Constable had a small wife he called Love.
Love would crouch at the back of the barn, waiting.
Love, he would call, Love, feeling about
With the aid of a longish, lit taper.
Sometimes he would fall.
Sometimes he would stumble over the straw.
This was months before he painted a picture called
Constable's *Hay Wain.*

Constable had a lovely child. It never stopped shouting.
Day and night its mouth was open, expelling air
   and much else.
Love would chase after it, laughing.
John would be there too, crying.
They ran across the fields, all three,
Until they grew distant as tiny memories.
A little later John painted a spike
At the bottom of a field.
He called it *Salisbury Cathedral*
   for the sheer hell of living.

Marcel Duchamp in conversation

I must give reasons, several I assume,
For the general conduct of my life.
It is a question of the spirit, of course,
The angle of that spirit to the world.
Generals need no longer die on horseback.
Painters, similarly, have no absolute obligation
To die at the easel.
What do I do in this world? you ask me.
You have any human's right to know.
I busy myself with my time.

Here, let us say, is an object, a thing.
I take it in my hand.
I do nothing but turn it and turn it about.
What does that achieve?
It gives the object an expressive vocation,
An effect. In short, it changes its destiny.

I, the son of a notary from Normandy,
Have sat down on my hat
For the unadulterated pleasure of the gesture.
There is more of this sort of thing:
I wear a red shirt;
I smoke ten havanas a day;
I go out little;
I see few friends;
I detest museums.

I am nothing but a prototype.
To everything that rushes past me I oppose
My own unshakeable serenity.
The fact is that there is no solution
Because there is no problem.
I know nothing of art and artists.
I know nothing of all that stuff.
I flow.
I bubble up from the spring.
I am that spring.

Edward Gibbon on the shores of Lac Leman,
December 1791

The winter is severe, with few balls
And little but my own correspondence to attend to.
All is darkness and anarchy in these days,
And I, Edward Gibbon Esq.,
Author of six volumes in quarto,
Am inclined towards the dropsical.

Good Madeira, I say, is essential
To my health and reputation.
May your hogshead prove as good as the last!
May it not be intercepted by the rebels or the Austrians!
I am in need of it badly.

And what of that *ci-devant* Kingdom of France?
You ask. Well may you ask it.
There is so much to say that I shall say nothing.
Except that I shall say this:
The world is in a state of dissolution,
And the French ladies are well settled
By the shores of Lac Leman.
They are companionably charming...

Otherwise, I shall expect no less
Than three pipes at least,
Of excellent Madeira in cask,
Together with some dozens of Malmsey Madeira.
Consign it to Messrs. Romberg, Voituriers
At Ostend. Give me timely notice of its march.
Let me live and die by my Madeira.

Prayer that I might ascend to paradise with my angels

after the French of Francis Jammes

When, at the last, I am obliged to take that journey, Lord,
Make it a day when the countryside is at its best,
All rouged with fragile poppies, and done up to the nines.
Let me choose my favourite path to you,
Illuminated by stars in the purest of skies.

Staunch stick in hand, I shall say to those donkeys,
My faithful companions:
I am no less than the poet Francis Jammes,
And I am on my way to Paradise,
That place where no hell shall disturb my rest
(for that, may the Good Lord's name be blessed).
Come, sweetest friends of this wren's-egg-blue sky,
You poor souls who, with a random switch of the ear,
Can so ably shrug off a blow, a bee, a fly...

Good Lord, make it possible for me to arrive
With my donkeys, and not on my own,
And ask your angels, when they see us ascending
Towards the light from the bottom of earth's stony path,
To approach us peaceably, leading us gently on
To clear streams above which cherries hang,
Sweet as the flushed flesh of girls who smile and dream,
And then, like my donkeys coming swaying on behind,
May I too bend my head, and be mirrored in
The limpidity of your eternal love
Until Time itself shall have no ending.

A faint dusting of blue hair

To be rid of it all at last.

To have thrown away the house, the furniture,
and all those uncertain griefs.

To walk away with nothing but one's own
peculiar lurching walk for company.

To have donated skin and bone
to the flayer and the anatomist.

To have pledged the organs elsewhere,
goodness knows how many years before.

To have chosen a particular plot in the boneyard,
and then to pass over it, light of step,
on the way to the coast.

To be scattered idly, here and there,
depending on the whim of some frolicsome wind.

Not to utter one word of complaint
if scarcely anything hits the road.

To become entangled in the blue hair
of stout-thighed women, fresh from the salon.

To see them blowing the dust of a lifetime
off their spectacles, and not to care one whit
if they think it talc, sawdust or worse.

Stranger in Paris

It is columnar, and entirely made of ice.

I cannot run away from it fast enough -
  the swifter I go, the sooner I arrive.

There is no speech in its mouth -
  merely the faint washings of bad breath.

The whole of it falls on top of me at all times.
That is why I must stay still beneath this bed.

I blow its name out into the air. It forms into
large and unwieldy chunks of volcanic rock.

If I were to collect up all the spoons
from all the cafes, I would never walk.

If I were a trickle, I could merge
into its waters - those canals, that river,
the open sore of all those sewers.

I fling my windows wide - rue des Augustins -
onto truth, righteousness, evil.
Everything is expanding on all sides...

Fine, grey pencil-strokes of rain fall slantwise
across the canvas of the sky, evasively.
Half of my face is wet - I may be crying.
The other half stays bone-dry.

In the courtyard below, six half-men circle
Two magnolia trees with wet, gleaming leaves,
Speaking in half-voices.
How can half-voices seem so fierce?

My words don't tell enough.
They shed their secrets sparingly.
Things get as far as the edge.
Then they draw back again.

There is nothing for me here.
My hands have become separated from my body.
My head lolls, as if thirsty for the basket.
Ask it. Ask it.

Paris, I say, Paris, now come to me.
Somewhere a blanket shifts, a train snorts.
Here is a brick. There - somewhere over there -
Is the sea. *Willingly.*

Before that day of days

Before the day of the burial,
   he was deep beneath the ground,
Questing for he knew not what, not knowing
   quite how far he would travel.
Before the day of the burial,
   he had said his long and short goodbyes to them all -
  to the rankness of the bedroom; her uncertain smile;
   all those small, lost tokens of happiness.

Before the day of the burial,
   he was already staring quietly at himself,
Seeing himself divested of himself,
   cleansed of all temporal violence.
Before the day of the burial,
   he enumerated one or two old memories -
there was nothing worth the keeping;
   they were all walking away.

Before the day of the burial,
   his voice had declined to a breathy whisper,
And his mouth was no more than a hole in the head.
Before the day of the burial,
   his limbs were stiffened and shrunken,
   and his movements were no more than a spasmodic judder.

Before the day of his death, he was already dead.

The broken bed

Imagine for yourselves the yawning miseries
of a broken bed. Examine in the cold light of a
winter's day the pressing need for hammers, a
bradawl, pliers, screwdrivers, a multiplicity of
brass-headed screws, and an infinity of small
acts of patience.

Observe yourself looking for the wood-block that
will faithfully support one failed corner of the
bed during this prolonged period of sweat-soaked
tinkering.

Consider just how many different shapes and sizes
of wood-block you will need to find before your
hand and eye alight upon the correct one.

Sit down on the floor and roll from buttock to
buttock as you watch yourself tearing from room
to room in pursuit of large plasters to staunch
the flow of the blood from those index fingers.

Pity yourself for being obliged to observe
yourself in such dire straits.

Now think twice before initiating that small
tease of an argument against those opponents of
whale-culling tonight, those few words tossed
down in the early evening, by a failing light,
that are set to combust, by bed-time, into
something of truly symphonic proportions, the
consequences of which will be, for the next
several weeks or so, a half-empty bed that you
will, during the few hours of reason that are
spared you, be striving in vain to be mending.

Transformation

I am much lighter and brighter than I used to be.
I leave no footprints in the mud of the garden.
My voice no longer growls and grates
 like a beast without speech or conscience.
Now it skims and flies along, flutingly.
The grip of my hand is like a breath of air
 on the palm.
I can answer the most difficult of questions:
Who made the world?
Who sits on the right hand of god the father?
Which angelic being is said to be
 the very embodiment of evil?
I am no longer fazed when darkness falls
 across the land,
And bodies pile up in grisly heaps.
I have no use for food, beds, scholarly instruction
Or public and private methods of transportation.
It is as if I have known everything that I needed
 to know from the very beginning.
You do not recognise me as your son any more -
 which makes me happy.
You wonder at me when I reply to you
 in the tongue of a stranger.
Where did he learn such talk? I hear you asking
 yourself, though you never speak the words
 out loud.
One day I will be gone from my room forever.
One day you will read about me in a book.
Cherish that book. It will be the key to the kingdom.

Best wishes

Take this wall away.
Let the house blow open to the sky.
Nothing much matters to me now.

Here are: jewellery, pens, letters.
Are your pockets large enough?
There must be others who need
To read, write or wear such things.
They are surplus to my needs.

Would a garden fall
Within the compass of your ambitions?
I have grown violets, daffodils, anemones,
All brave portents of spring.
You may need such portents yourself.
Have this fistful with my best of wishes.
Now I must go.

And good luck with the world.

Piecing it all together

There was a hand.
And a quota of blood on that hand.
But I had expected an arm.

There was an ear,
And something encrusting that ear.
But I had expected a face.

There was a leg,
And, loosely attached, some brown string.
But I had expected a foot.

Yes, I had expected
Each levelling piece
In its old, proper place...

Yesterday, to my joy and my sorrow,
All these parts came together,
And he spoke to me,

Greeted me here, elbow to elbow...
Was it done yet? he said, shifting the coals.
Well, whatever...

And there we all were, he and she,
Jumping backwards, like children,
Into the eternal verities of spring-time
In the sun-blenched Carpathians...

Few things happen

Few things happen at the height of summer.
Eyes squint up at the sun.
Pages of books are turned.
Laughter threads its way between the trees.

Few things happen at the height of summer.
The angle of a sunshade is adjusted.
Someone loses the midge swat.
Many glasses are raised.

Few things happen at the height of summer.
A vehicle creeps noiselessly to the door.
A man strides up with a bag.
The family sighs.

Ashes are carelessly scattered
In the general direction of autumn.

His journeyings

Locally, he extracted food -
Such as a juniper berry or two -
From places set long and wide apart,
Picking his way through snagging scrub
      and small, mean alleys,
Attending to horse flies with wild flittings of his fingers
As he invaded, ever blundering,
Those many private walks he had committed
So easily to memory throughout the long days
Of his hopeless and ceaseless journeyings.

When asked to sing, his voice came out
Long and thin and distant,
Then in quick, staccato bursts of shrill piping,
As if one voice was not widely known to the other.
It was then that he would stare down at his fingers,
As if to find there some ready animal proof
Of his wayward compulsions.
His fingers lay lean and still and neatly serried,
Fond, wounded victims in a world of some hospital
Whose address he had perhaps wilfully misremembered,
Though he knew, as he stared, how pallid and how watery
      the light was in that ward,
And how heavily the dust lay
      on those several crimped coverlets...

When they came to find him,
He was curled neatly in on himself,
On some lush diamond of chance grass,
      quietly, for protection.
And there was nothing else by
      except a random strew of berries
      fresh issued from his mouth,
And that single horse fly,
So proud and so watchful, as it hung about his eye...

He who blasted it to eternity
Gave it scarcely more than a moment's attention.

The pledge

This is a day like no other. A sword has fallen into my hand.
All this cityscape will soon be level ground,
As level as the plane of this my down-turned hand.
Amidst a jumble of arms and legs I rummaged and fumbled,
	looking for the perfect fit.
That stranger's last breath was how I knew I had come alive.

I was a meek man once. Now I am a tower of flame.
The gifts I offer are scattered in such abundance.
Not a soul on this barren earth has the right to refuse.
When I walk out of this door, all the flowers bow down.
I sing to myself, and the birds choir with me.
I say to myself: holy are these names which I utter.
They will run from generation to generation.

My sweet daughter takes my hand when I fall back into my chair.
She kisses it. She tastes the sharpness of salt on my palm.
I bless her with words she will never understand.
They are like music to me. I sit astride each stave.
I propel myself heavenward.

This is a day like no other, I say.
A sword has fallen into my faltering hand.

The frustrations of Melopes

A tuneless lyre still makes its point,
Thought Melopes, stirring the dust
Of centuries with stiff, young toes.
I love her still, though cry she must.

Melopes woke up with a shout.
The lyre was broken, on the floor.
The window gave on nothingness -
Cat-stink, ordure, much as before.

When she approached, she seemed to float.
His fingers fumbled with the strings.
When music reaches out to girls,
Even the coldest beauty sings...

Kratikos

Kratikos, that boy on the rock,
Peering into the water,
Kratikos... Who gave him such eyes?
Who modelled those ankles?

Kratikos, emerging from here,
How could it be possible?
Scion of a slut and a cobbler,
Who nurtured such beauty?

Kratikos, dead now six years -
Some mishap on water.
Kratikos, who hated you so?
Who snuffed out your candle?

Ceremony

Each life has a small, proportionate smile allotted to it.
The smile itself is preserved in a trim jade box.
Each man keeps his box beneath a bed impregnated with musk.
A smile can live in the dark for as long as it must.

Each life has a small, proportionate
                          movement attached to it.
Usually this is a reaching out with a single hand.
When the movement is done with, it may be tidied away.
Now the life can sit quietly,
                          in expectation of another day.

Each life has a small, proportionate wish allotted to it.
The wish may concern goodness, health or longevity.
Each man has his choice, but there is no turning back.
If longevity is his wish, the backbone must not crack.

The bedrooms

The bedrooms are lonely at this time of day.
No one is present to care for them.
All the night things are in disarray.
Windows look out onto windows.
Occasional cars move down in the street.
Inside, it is all stillness and silence.
There is an obscure absence of feet.

The bedrooms are lonely at this time of day.
The novels are closed, the tissues balled in the bin.
All the sounds are on the outside, looking in.
Coverlets stare blindly at pillows.
Pyjamas pose awkwardly on the bed.
There is a quiet thirsting for something.
It feels like a land of the dead.

The bedrooms are lonely at this time of day.
There is no urgency to the ticking of the clock.
The pink vanity box is locked.
The sun does a little idle splashing.
Dust gives a light skim to the sheets.
Across town, in a room full of shoulders and noise,
Some man daydreams of silence, and sleep.

Laying the shadows down

Shabby days, one heaped upon another.
The autobiography, steadfastly unfinished.
Every so often, an ice cream, guzzled greedily.
Then: Prokofiev. With tea.

Her call, ringing in the bedroom.
I am out again, I smile to myself.
Someone is laying the shadows down with a plumb line.
A match flares in that restaurant, beside the sea.

When I walk, it is with a purpose.
When I look, it is in order to see.
Three books a week. Double whiskies in the evening.
Bach. Brahms. Prokofiev. The three. *The three.*

Owning the sea

Yesterday a man said he owned the sea.
We pleaded with him: give it back to the earth!
He insisted it was his, by right of birth.

Yesterday the people killed a man
Who'd said he owned the sea, for his arrogance,
For the way he spoke, and the way he swayed above us all.
They chopped him down, then up - heart, fingers, balls.

Yesterday a voice said it owned the sea.
We stood above the spot, staring down at cold earth.
We dug and dug, took parts of him, flung them about.
Now the voices come from everywhere -
                                        tiny, insistent shouts.

To friendship

Nothing lasts as the stones last.
The flower crumples in the hand.
The face fades in the memory.
The smile is wiped by the cold.

The love is lost on the next corner.
The building sighs to a smoke of rubble.
The gods age with the years.
The match dies in the damp room.

The sword rusts in the rain.
The wish dissolves in the stream.
The laughter sours to a bullet.
The lace of the shoe is broken.

The meat reduces to rottenness,
The cat to a heap of old bones.
And even the emperor comes down
To a risible pizzle.

The unit of measurement

I was always the last in their thoughts,
Their smallest unit of measurement.

If a smaller gift could have been found,
That is the gift they would have given me.

If, by some miracle, I could have survived
Without food, drink or clothing,
They would have dispensed with such things.

Had they been under no obligation
To speak to me,
To teach me my letters,
To demonstrate to me
How to set one foot in front of another,
They would not have done so.

Had there been a smaller space in which to pen me,
They would have found it.
They would have put me there.

Had they not died, so expeditiously, at my hand,
I would have died in their stead.
They would have seen to it.

I was always the last in their thoughts,
Their smallest unit of measurement.

The running bridegroom

Then the bridegroom was gone from them.
They sought him out in every darkest corner.
His picture had vanished from the walls.
Even his footsteps, hurrying away,
        were an ever receding memory.

The bride sat, slumped, in the parlour,
        counting her tears,
One for every day of their briefest of brief engagements.
The mother clattered the pans.
The father, fuming and fretting, pulled on his beard...

Meanwhile, the bridegroom gathered pace as he ran.
He spread his arms wide to embrace the newly risen sun.
He sang as he ran, and others sang with him:
Bridegroom oh bridegroom, they sang, *whither are you roaming?*

A blessing, in kind

In the place of unstinting effort,
He offered indolence of a very particular kind -
To lie flat in the bedroom,
Observing the dust motes rise;
To hear their voices, rhyming and chiming,
From across the hall,
Seeming to offer him nothing at all;
To see that paper at which he stared,
Day in, day out,
Willing words to gush from his pen, and then...
Altogether it was too much to contemplate.
Words were always too hard to find.
So, in place of unstinting effort,
He gave back to the world
Indolence of a very particular kind.
And the world blessed him, in kind.

Delicate skimming motions

Late in the day, just moments before the light died,
He saw the creature moving across the pond -
A kind of delicate, slow, skimming motion.
When he raised his voice to it, though none too harshly,
It disappeared. Then just a question mark hung in the air.
It felt a little like a song.

The next day, at that same, small hour of recessive light,
He crouched beside the pond, behind a deck chair,
Holding his breath. It was a test, he felt.
If the creature were to come today,
        it would be a message of some kind.

There was some beauty in the thing, no doubting that,
The way it glided, first backwards, then sideways,
The way it held out what looked like an arm -
        or perhaps a wing...
It had wanted to be there at that time
Because it knew of him in some past life, in some past time...

It did not come, so in memory of the thing,
He disrobed himself, and moved across the pond,
Trying to rise above it all,
In a delicate skimming motion,
So that he might be observed,
By the creature itself perhaps, or his own wife,
At worst.

Whose image is this?

The face on the coin was his own face.
The light in the candle was his.
The stars belonged in his pocket.
He felt emboldened to give

Of the millions he was grasping,
Of the coins that were spilling around.
He tossed them all gaily skyward.
The stars shone, metallically proud.

They formed a small circle to watch him.
They seized all his marvellous gifts.
They stared at the coins from his pocket.
Yes, that face on the coin was his...

They melted the coins from his pocket
By the light of a million stars.
They buried him deep in the bogland.
Their spades rang, metallically hard.

Those last words

Lastly we spoke of love and of its vanishing.
How it had come so suddenly and, just as suddenly,
                              left again.
We spoke in small whisperings, as if ashamed.
We spoke hurriedly, as if to be done
                              with such treasonable matter.
When the wind came on, we huddled a little closer together.
The closer we huddled, the more the words
                              seemed to fall away.

And then it was day.

An interruption at the bakery

He had the word Homeric on his tongue's tip,
And with it came a certain lengthening of the body
As it rose from the chair,
A particular lift of the chin,
And an unearthly manner of walking,
From porch direct to bakery,
Which somehow outpaced, with such accustomed ease,
The efforts of that collective Other
That was gathered, in a mean, small huddle,
For mere food's sake, at the closed shop door...

As he stood there, musing and sipping
At antiquity's bottomless pitcher,
A child squeezed at his knee -
Doubtless some orphaned son
Of one of sad Patroclus' former attendants.

Prayer

Let it not happen as it may once have happened.

Let it take a different tack,
Into the parching winds of the deepest South,
Or out beyond the rampant snows of the North-West.

Let the feet rise with confidence,
Each step firmly taken,
With a whistle to gather up the intimacies of friends.

Let the foodstuffs be prepared, clothes washed,
Features sluiced to perfection.

Let the teeth be set firm and white and brilliant -
As befits such a quest.

Let all the knowledge be shared beforehand,
The greater schemes and the lesser whisperings.

Let all the handshakes be done with, the vows exchanged,
The last valedictory slappings of the back.

Let the beers be drunk down to the dregs,
The wills solemnised, and the children blessed
With a word or two of the politest wisdom known to man.

Above all things else,
Let it not happen as it may once have happened.

Extremities

Extremes of hope are married to extremes of sorrow.
You lost your way in the winds and the rain.
Someone out there cut a bare chunk of ice,
And presented it to me with some degree of ceremony.
It had your footprint embedded within it.
I stared at your photograph on the wall tonight.
It blared out at me like a speaking trumpet,
And then, all of a sudden, the light fell,
And you were gone from me.

On the days that I snap my fingers at you,
You feign a slow death of sorts,
Lolling forward like a leaf before the sink.
It is that old sink of which I speak,
The one it took two grown men to carry.
You touched its edge before it soared,
Backwards-flipping, into the skip.
It was a sink of old suds and older memories.

When we chance to marry again,
On that grown day of sunlight and sorrow,
I shall take your hand and point to some distant horizon.
And there you will be waiting,
Beckoning and waving, waving and beckoning,
Until my arm tires at the very thought of it.

Danceable tunes

Danceable tunes for the earliest hours,
Out on the pavement with bare legs flying,
Danceable tunes for the peaceable neighbours,
And for the roarers too,
Nail-biting souls of tar-smeared doors.

Quickening thoughts for the dullards' ears,
Words to enlighten, words to console,
Making the dead rise up, float in a convoy,
Down past the duck pond,
Over the steepening climb of our hills.

Words and tunes in good neighbourly measures,
Scrapings of the bow, ululations of the throat,
Hands grasped, necks twisted, hair back-flying,
With hard cold coming on. The whole world aches.

Her clarinet's abiding sweetness

for Jesse

She struck a note so high and so extreme
That every body in the entire wide world
Lurched back a pace or two,
And then she proceeded to pursue them all,
Taunting, pushing, corralling them
    into the smallest corner imaginable.

They stayed there, with pent breath,
For seven thousand years
As she paused to change her reed.

Then with that new reed came a new note
Of abiding sweetness.
That shadowy corner fell away,
And all the peoples of the world
    were once again free
        to mingle amongst themselves.

The soldiers

There are many lines of soldiers here,
Standing stock-still just in front of my door.
I do not know what they have come for.
I do not know how long they have been here.

The tallest presses a petition into my hand,
But I lack the language to understand it.
The lines towards the back are growing restless now.
There is a stomping of feet, a clearing of throats.
I hear a rousing tune rising from somewhere.

I do not know how many hours, how many days
I may have to stand here.
I do not know what they want from me.
And, as I examine them one by one,
He with the wind-combed hair,
And another who looks gently askance,
I do not know what I want from myself.

Loneliness

I have tried to define the nature of loneliness.
And then I have abandoned that quest,
Preferring instead to walk alone in the garden,
To throw a stick, or examine the progress of a stream.

Upon returning to the house,
The quest begins once again -
I stare at a portrait on the wall,
I count the knives in the drawer,
I examine that odd reflection of myself
In some hand-me-down silver spoon.

When the wind leans against the side of the house,
I listen for a car and, at last,
The gate creaks, and I hear it approaching,
With such stealth, across the tarmac.
When the door opens, we embrace.
I stare into the face
    of loneliness.

Resignation

I am the smallest of the lost continents.
I sank beneath the sea the day your back was turned.
Now, when you look out upon that great expanse of waters,
It is just as if I have never been -
Seagulls float and skim so easily above the place where I sank;
The winds comb the waters as if they have nothing to hide
             and nothing to reveal...

I have no idea what I shall do down here
During the aeons of time which lie ahead of me.
Plants will grow upon me at their whim,
Upon which tiny suckerfish will doubtless feed.

Every decade or so a boat will settle down here to join me.
There will be no conversation between us.
No distant lost cries will reach me.
Frankly, there will be nothing to be said.

My prayer

I pray for an end to all of this.

That the sunlight will enfold me,
And a word soothe my raging itches.

That a vision will reach me
Of lightly dimpled fingers touching my cheek.

That her voice, once again,
Will meander through the courtyard.

That my mother will tell me that story once again,
The one she always told me.

That there will be an apple, heavy in the hand,
And a word of whispered hope in my ear.

That the wind will blow when the light falls,
Lifting the hem of her garment.

That she will still approach me from some great distance,
Pretending not to look.

That I will know the limits of my life,
Where I once began, and whither I am tending.

That it will not be this wall again when I raise my head,
And its shadow across my ankle.

That I will know my name and my nature,
That my voice will sound, and my breathing come even.

That I will not rise up and walk when they tell me to,
For every dying moment of my occluded life.

A serene slippage of anchor

There were countless opportunities for walking slowly again -
Beside that bend in the river
        just before nightfall, for example,
As those candles finally guttered, having withstood,
Thanks to our cupped hands, the very worst of the winds.

No, you needn't ask for sudden explanations. There are none.
This is my sole voice speaking to you here. The rest is echo.
Ask of me what you will then. I will absorb your questions.
Nothing will prove too difficult in this situation.

If she had approached him as in former times, side-long,
With raised hands shielding her against the glare of the sun,
He would surely have thought differently of her.
He would have known her for the person he had once recognised.
There would have been left to him more than that single shoe,
        that ragged handkerchief.

Lead me up the stairs as far as they lead.
Your handshake has something of the familiar about it.
You call this a room, the one I am just about to enter.
You call these people, strewn across the benches.
They are mere tokens of life, straw-men,
        all with the heads of horses.

Now that I have been invited, I shall sweetly stay.
Nothing constrains me to do otherwise on this day of days.
I have had my fill of greetings. They were personable enough
        for the most part.
The dock is receding from me. We have all slipped anchor again.
Why don't you pray for me now as I always invited you to do?

The visitor

Set your glass down on the nearest surface if you must.
The sound of glass shattering always sets my teeth on edge.
Now we are alone together in this room, it seems,
And you say we need to become familiar again.
Did you really say you knew me once, when we were quite young?
That we held hands at some railway station on the East Coast?
It may be someone else you are referring to.
I have no memory of having met you before.
I always remember voices, and voices do not change.

Why are you crying now over there?
I have said nothing that is even remotely insensitive.
I have merely denied that I ever met you.
I tell you once again: I recognise the sounds of voices.
They never leave me. What is more I recognise faces, bodies too,
And you - you - I have never seen before,
Not until this afternoon, when you walked up the drive,
        uninvited,
And asked to be welcomed at my birthday party.
Yes, you had flowers in your hand.
You told me my age.
You behaved, right from the beginning,
As if you were familiar to me.

But the fact is that we have never met before,
And that you must have gleaned all this information
        from goodness knows where.
I asked you to leave before the last light died -
        we have only so many candles in this house.
I asked you, politely, to leave with all the others.
And I thought that you had left.
I thought that I was all alone in the house.
That is why I locked the door, and took myself off to bed.
That is why I switched off the porch light.
How can you persist so much in being here?
How can you tell me that you have always shared my life
When I know you to be a complete stranger to me?

That was the day

He took her by the hand, very loosely, very gently,
As one would grasp the hand of a child.
He led her, this way and that,
As far as the rose arbour, and then back again
To the shadow of the kitchen door.

He spoke to her of his life,
And then he asked about hers,
Nodding at each faltering word,
Smiling with the full benevolence
Of the sun across her golden hair.

He gave her tea in a chipped mug,
A biscuit or two.
He showed her photographs of himself, his wife,
When they were young and in
The full abundance of their strength.

He lifted her up at an upstairs window,
To show her how the fields fell away beyond the marsh,
And then he released her from the porch
Like something small and mechanical,
Wending its way, back and forth,
Down that long and ever receding stretch of country lane.

Yes, that was the day.

The moment

There is to be no relenting.
There is no time for such things.
The whole point is to drive on ahead,
Without pause or faltering.

There is to be no waiting, no hesitation,
And no idle clack-clacking of tongues.
To walk in silence is the order.
That is your oath, and that is your bond.

In the past we dealt with reasons -
The multiple issues of causation,
The shadow-play of ideologies,
The ever-shifting patterns of the years.

We examined, minutely,
How entire civilisations rose,
And then fell again.
Now we are the ones.
Set aside your fears.

A man called No One

A man called No One knocks at the door.
It is February time, a sharp snap of cold in every crevice.
Breath hangs in the air like old, thin curtains.
I am at a loose end, whether to stay or to go. Which.

It is then that No One calls, and I let him in
        with a modicum of ceremony.
I plump up the cushion and he settles, glad to be somewhere.
It is so easy for No One to be Nowhere.
He spends his lifetime in such parts, he tells me.
Until today, he tells me, when such a blessing
        fell from the air.

To be welcomed into the house of a stranger!
That the door should be unlatched,
        and the man turn as he enter!
Usually, he tells me, it is a matter of the blank-faced stare
And maybe a slight, uneasy shuffling of feet,
        which says just the one thing:
Something may be afoot here, but darned if I can say what it is.

I tell him then. I tell him straight.
I knew nothing of his coming.
The door was unlatched through a roaring fit of forgetfulness.
I have welcomed him into my house for want of anything better,
        that is the sad truth of it, I tell him.
We both sit opposite each other, heads hung, keening,
        like limp black tulips in a fluted vase.

Advice

If the alarm should ring, ignore it.
Live on as quiet as you were.
Make a sanctuary of yourself.
Hug yourself a little. Care.

Walk familiar streets with caution.
Don't be quick to meet the eye.
Be regular in all your habits.
When the hour strikes, assent to die.

Do not share much with your neighbour.
A match perhaps. One candle. Tea.
Let words be sparse, the flesh unclasped.
Practise your trade, covertly.

Heap paper upon quiet paper.
Sharpen your pencil in the dark.
Scrutinise the latest message.
Smile widely at what you think you thought.

Walk the seven streets with caution.
Never meet a stranger's eye.
Never vary in your habits.
Be prepared, always, to die.

The song of the three fish

I saw three fish descend the stairs,
Arm in arm and devil-may-care,
Singing some old-time fishers' song
Of cruel men with hooks and prongs

Who pitched and tossed on the bucking waves
In boats as tough as those men were brave,
And stabbed at long-dead, helpless friends,
Hauling them forth on the prong's sharp end -

Such lean and comely fishermen,
All bronzed by toiling in the sun,
With fingers strong as an yron vise,
And eyes that flashed, and tongues of ice...

They sang and sang as down they came,
All wet from the sea, and wildly gay.

The box

When those young men came on down the road,
Carrying that box on their shoulders,
Pushing their way through the traffic,
Determined to get to, at once,
Wherever it was that they were going,
I understood nothing of what they were doing
Until our car had passed on by,
And, moving away from them up a rising slope,
I could gain some prospect on their fears, their hopes,
As they hurried away from us at such speed,
That so solid phalanx of heaving backs, legs, shoulders,
Carrying that box above their heads,
That poor, decrepit, filthy, lidless box, entirely full,
I could see it now, of something all wrapped in white,
Being jostled and even thrown
Beside all that blaring and buffeting of the road.

It was some mother's son that they were carrying
To its final resting place,
I could see that now
Through the besmirched back windscreen of the car,
It was some mother's son who was being jostled
And almost thrown
Amidst all that filthy, midday, Cairo heat.

Cutting a knife through the daylight

I was not ready for your approaches.
My lamp was lost in the cellar, rusting.
The oil was all spent.
These clothes were unwashed.

And yet still you extended a hand to me.
And when you did that,
My lamp was burnished until it shone,
The oil brimmed over,
My clothes looked fresh-bought from the store.

The street is alive now to welcome us.
Any bride and any groom -
And today it is the two of us, arms locked steadily -
Will cut a knife through the daylight.

My sufferings

I suffer for the small things of life.
I suffer for the plants and the flowers.
And I suffer for your hand, limp in sleep.

A little later I will suffer
For the aroma of coffee rising
From the apartment beneath me.
My nostrils will quiver with the sadness of it all.

Then I will suffer for myself,
For the fact that I stand here in this room,
Waiting, shoeless,
Watching you - you - asleep beneath me,
Without a single thought for all my sufferings,
Asleep or waking,
Today, yesterday or forever.

I own the sufferings of a beast.

Borrowing a coat

No one misunderstands a coat
Worn in a very particular way -
Some holiday mood perhaps -
On the kind of day
When the world wills us to be outdoors,
Walking the streets, the hills, the moors,
Gulping in the biting air, all at once,
Until we are about to burst,
Or shout hosannah to the skies...

No, no one misunderstands us then -
Least of all the man
By whom the coat was lent,
He who shivers alone, indoors,
With his megrims and his cramps,
And his low-toned hums,
Counting, obsessively, from one to ten,
Then down again,
Like some arthritic, slow-stairs-descent,
From ten to one.

Each single bullet makes its mark.
No one denies the pain of loss.
Tuesday, a little after nine.
Numbering the children, all in line.

Renee, Amelia, Jack, Siobhan.
Naming the children, all in line.
Each careful bullet made its mark.
No one denies the pain, the cost.

Fallen, her kerchief, in the yard.
His face, pressed close, against the screen.
Counting the bullets, one by one:
Amelia's, Renee's, Jack's, Siobhan's...

So clean, each bullet hits its mark,
Sliding from here to eternity,
One swift, clean motion - like a dream,
Some dream of hatred on a screen.

One scream, Amelia's. Jack, Siobhan
Look round, see nothing but his arm
Cocked in defiance, steadily -
Some dream of hatred, cold, serene.

Renee, Amelia, Jack, Siobhan -
Remember them. Stare at the screen,
The very screen he stared at then.
The bullets fly, eternally.

Renee, Amelia, Jack, Siobhan -
Naming the children, one by one.
No one denies the pain, the cost.
No one denies the pain of loss.

Cold Street

I live on a street called Gladness.
There is always some hand reaching out.
My work takes me downhill, to Cold Street.
They are muffled down there. They don't talk.

It is hard for me to travel.
I live two quite separate lives.
The smiles that I use in the evening
The daylight people spit out.

I shall move one day to Cold Street.
For me, there is no other way.
It is where I must surely settle.
I have seen it every day.

I have seen them drift, as if dreaming,
Carrying all that they have -
A bundle of clothes and two blankets,
Looking so wretchedly sad.

From Gladness to sadness, they whisper.
Down Cold Street they chant, every day:
This is where you must one day settle.
Come, child, there is no other way.

The paper lantern

Her face was a paper lantern in the Chinese style -
Just imagine that. I took it with me everywhere,
Swinging it from the finger of one hand
Through the smallest and twistiest back alleys
To light my way.
                  Later I would hang it above my table
In that restaurant which borders the canal.
It shed the warmest glow of red light,
Perfectly illumining the rondure of my plate.
Do I call that fate?

In bed at night, it lay within easy reach of where I lay,
Collapsed flat now, beside my book, biding its time.
Though the light was gone now, I could see it still
In my inner eye,
                  and then you would float free of your lantern
And dance for me. I would watch you, eyes closed,
Doing one of your slow and delicate turns.

Your voice would rise like a warm puff of red smoke
In the air, moving in the tiniest of arabesques,
You and your smoke together,
                  the smoke of your voice rising,
The turn of your heel forever, lighting my way
Beside the canal to my table, hovering above my chair,
Above my menu, inviting me to please sit down, sir,
Illumined by your presence forever,
In that Chinese restaurant I loved so much,
The only one in the city.

The fine balance

What you need is the finest of fine balances,
Something fabricated so carefully
By a small man in a basement workshop,
Good with eye and hand, who will bend over all day,
Testing and weighing each small part,
And when all is dusted and done,
Oil cog, wheel, needle, sprocket,
With a tiny droplet of oil, first smoothed across
The ball of his littlest finger
So that everything, by and by, will roll steadily on.

And when all that is over and done,
You must lift it with such care and gentleness -
Using both hands - and place it in the waiting vitrine,
In the cool of the day, way beyond
The invasive stare of the sun.

Now organise it in there with the care
That each part deserves: first place your balance
In the corner, at the very edge of the table,
And then, beside it, the man himself, still cross-legged,
And with hands still poised to make
Those last finely tuned adjustments at the end of the day.
Then all will go well, and you will sleep happily
In your bed - which must be positioned -
Don't forget this - no more than one metre
To the south of the table,
Within nodding distance of that old man's head.

The perfect time to write

No time to write this now.

Write it later, when day is more fully to hand.
Write it when voices flood in from everywhere.
Write it when meat is heaped up in abundance.
Write it when you are listening out for the words,
       leaning across the table,
       eyes staring into my eyes,
       seeing nothing.

Write it when nothing else stands between me
       and all the words
       I am ready to pour out to you.
Write it when there is an eager expectation that words
Will be sufficient and more for just the two of us.
Write it when words are suspended here in the air before me,
       waiting to be snatched at,
       waiting to be caught in a net,
       waiting to be weighed and bartered.

Write it when words are the only things on offer,
When the entire landscape seems to have withered away.
Write it when the days consume me, and the nights oppress me,
And the afternoons are longer than the inching of shadows
       across the pool.
Write it when, all of a sudden, the ears close down,
       the mouth clogs, and the stomach fills with bile.

Write it when bent double, when stretched on the rack,
       or on the beach.
Write it when your hand is a stranger to your thoughts,
When you watch your hand moving as if it had dared to be
Everything that you had chosen to avoid in your life.
Yes, write it then.

To me.

The verification of a presence

There is too much light in this street.
Please switch off the sun for an hour or two.
I prefer to grope around in cooling darkness.
There is such excitement in not knowing.

There are too many people here.
One man is quite sufficient.
I am speaking of myself, of course.
I find myself such easy company.

Who is this bumping up against me in the dark?
Why does it squeak at me when spoken to?
Bring me a little light someone.
I need to verify the presence of this total stranger.

The haar

The sea-mist came bundling along that remote shore line
Like a ball of grey wool fresh fallen
      from my grandmother's needles.
I was ready with the nets just then,
      counting out the clams in an orderly fashion.

When the sea-mist enveloped me,
      I struck out to left and to right.
Even my hoarsest cries were seriously muffled.
There was nothing to free me from my discontent.
The clams, as a body, seeing their chance,
      returned to the waters.

I returned to the house with strands of lank sea-mist
      adorning my shoulders.
When my wife saw that my hands were empty,
      she enquired after the whereabouts of the nets,
      all four of them,
Each one the cost of an entire ancestral lifetime's
      hard toiling.
I made my excuses. I explained the situation.

Yet still I looked a little like Odysseus returning,
      when viewed, magnificently, across the shoulders.

Gathering the instances

I gather my own instances about me.
One has to do with days, and how they are numbered.
A second includes the lives of stars,
And my swimming presence amongst them.

When I have all my instances
Close pent in a circle about me,
I teach them a song
Common to the farthest flung reaches of civilisation.

You would be surprised with what joy they sing it.

Keys to locked doors

There are so many locked doors and so few keys.
There are so many locksmiths engaged upon
The thankless task of making
Thousand upon thousand of ill-fitting keys.

Each useless key is thrown into the river.
That night some swimmer dives, in the dark,
To reclaim it
Because metal is so precious.

There are so many locked doors,
And so many calling from behind those doors.
There are so many linguists engaged upon
The thankless task of deciphering
The languages they speak,
The thousand upon thousand who beat
Upon those closed locked doors.

Each useless language is quickly
Forgotten or abandoned,
Yet not by the children who play by the river.
New words keep issuing from their small, young mouths,
And each one sounds like a trickle of water,
Or the rusting key to a lock as yet undiscovered.

The note

He carried that single note inside his head
For the several months he spent
Exploring the mysteries of love-objects
He found ranged in small vitrines
Behind tall museum walls.

He wondered at each one he saw.
One was entirely straw, knotted and twisted up,
To make an ampersand of sorts.
What would they do with such a thing?
Hang it above the bed?
Or have someone shake it or wave it
Above human heads?

He had no love-objects in his life,
No intricate arrangements
Fashioned from straw, wool, wire,
Or any other material that might have come to hand.
Instead, he had that one long, sweet note
Calling to him, day in, day out,
Which, though a single note alone,
He construed, in his saddest moments, as a song.

Drunks, babies and two dogs

It was in some back room of a pub
Where he stood, reading his poems
To an audience of drunks, babies and two dogs.

The talk went on - his talk and theirs.
There was smoke spiralling up between the Toby Jugs.
The TV was on.

His voice was a song he heard,
And he kept it there, fixed inside his head,
Stuck straight and firm as a blade rammed into peat.

It cut through the voices in that place.
It made them all see
How words could sing like no other tune known to man,

More instantly recognisable, more true
Than the barking of a dog,
Or the quick hawking of a gob of spit into a spittoon.

The magistrates

The magistrates hold tightly in their arms
Worlds we had never known to sing about.
They rock them, highly, nimble on their feet.
Pale flowers are strewn, which keeps the occasion sweet.

The magistrates, those old men, muscled taut,
Sing about worlds long vanished from this world,
Strange, heightened places with viridian streams
Which soodle, winking at the brightest suns.

How can these men be magistrates? we ask.
How can they uphold laws when all we see
Are goat-like creatures, beckoning with their thumbs
To dance with them, and chatter mindlessly?

A summary

The wind is gathering in the pines.
I could not ask for more than this.
The spoon makes a gesture to the tea cup.
Answer my letter. Do not ignore me.

When the curtain falls, the applause is like thunder.
Rescue me from the abyss of my life.
The second drink chases, giggling, after the first.
She was the last to leave. And then the lights went off.

The spring refreshes like no other.
I would write to you had I words fit for the paper.
The rain dances on the pavement,
      cooling the edge of the lip.
Do not wait for me. Do not pretend to bother.

Naomi or Elizabeth

It was the most fragile of boats, I heard.
How could some vessel of clay and straw
Sustain her weight or keep out the sea?
It's all a mystery to me.
Yes, she was small,
But she was fully grown all the same,
Sitting at the prow,
Looking out for the other shore.
That's how I always imagine her.

And what was her name?
I knew it once, but it fell away,
As most things tend to fall away these days.
It was something plangent, I recall,
Like Naomi or Elizabeth,
Something to make a splash
When spoken out loud...
Now she is on the water,
And she has no need for a name
Because no one will be calling to her any more.
No one will recognise her for who she once was...

I think of her now as I knew her
When she was a girl.
There was something singular about her even then.
When we talked she would stay silent,
When we played our childish games,
She often did not join in.
Even then she dreamt of boats and water.
She would stare at pictures of the sea.
She would look across the sands of the desert -
We were entirely surrounded, it always seemed,
        by the drifting sands of the desert -
And imagine to herself all that her future might be.

Statement

I do not love what I cannot denounce.
That is in the nature of all contradictions.
Life throws its blessings down and around.
Sparks fly to the ceiling and beyond.

There is a wood beyond here, which makes its presence felt.
Pure poetry, they name it, chock full of ravening things.
I stir the pot. I make the groundlings squeal.
Voices are useless in an emptiness.

Lost lovers strewn like petals; dead, lost things
Found in some wood, with verses tacked to boughs,
Soon to be swallowed by the gulping air;
Dead voices, loving what they don't denounce.

Verses are useless in an emptiness.

A boy

for Joseph

Something has come at last of what we made.
This handsome, sturdy boy is craning round,
Taking the world in through his keen, small eyes.
His hands are grasping, upwards, at some cloud.

I push him, with due patience, through the streets.
He tries to tell me what he feels. I nod.
He thanks me with a smile. I give it back.
The pushchair's lurching now: *A dog! A dog!*

I raise him up. He's blocking out the sun.
He squirms against my shoulder - o giant slug,
Don't disappear just yet into the grass.
Pulse with your vital life upon this rug.

The experiment

He tore his small and impoverished life
to pieces, frenziedly, as if it were
some wretched, oil-soaked rag.

He tweaked up each bit, separately,
between his fingers and, with his
cigarette lighter, set fire to it,
with infinite care,
an infinity of patience...

Letting each one go with a 'pah!'
of exasperation and profound content
before it burnt his finger ends.

Three hundred and seventy four
bits of life in all, small incidents
and yet smaller still, including even
the tiniest: that faintest flicker
of an eyelash, on some night in November,
during the year of his birth...

And then he lay back, marmoreal-still,
having nothing to contemplate now
except the relentless horrors
of all that was still to come.

Vain pursuits

He who goes in pursuit of the proprieties of age
Must put behind him all thought of gardens
With their indolent, flush-faced blooms
And vain marquees;
Books too much fall away
Together with, needless to say,
Those keepsakes, now dead and dry,
Once so dearly interleaved...

Sufficient unto the day must be a stick,
Tall if you like, but thin and gnarled,
On which to lean; with which to prod and poke
At youthful misdemeanours glimpsed,
Mistily now, across some yard
Where lovely girls and boys
Giggle and point
At swishing sticks
Before returning to
The bloom of fleshly joys -
Veined, warm and soft at times,
Then cool, quick, hard.

The weight of them on the palm

She turned over the bricks in the field,
Combing them with the fork
As if they were hair.

She kicked the charred pot,
Smelled a remnant of smoke
From a bonfire of bones.

Home

She looked up to the mountains,
Saw the long shadows hurrying.
She wondered about the soul.

Then, picking up her skirts,
She moved to the cart, dreamily,
As if about to pass through a door

Which would lead into sunlight,
In an oval pool, on a chequered floor,
With a cluster of old, known faces,

And a child, fingering a necklace
Of smooth-turned stones.
Amber. The weight of them on the palm...

Home

Gratitude

I cannot thank you enough for being yourself.
It would have been so easy for you to be another.
In a different place. At a different time.
        Touching another's arm.
Instead, you are resigned to such life as you have.
I agree. It has not been easy.

When I took the scissors to the stems
        of the hollyhocks;
When I mistook the old world for the new;
When I set the baby going, doorward,
        like a clockwork mouse -
At such times, you re-considered it all.
You pulled out the bag from beneath the bed.

We have been wintering here since the knot was tied,
        summer and winter.
It is an old, tried knot now, small and hard
        as a frozen pea,
Beyond the reach of nimbler fingers.
When I stand in this doorway, and think of
        all we have achieved,
A great sea comes rushing towards me.

If you were to remove from this shelf
        everything that was yours,
What would be left to console me?
I am a model of frozen gratitude.
Do not except me.

Her emergence

During those long, slow hours before we met,
I was living in the room behind the tower.
It was a happy room, lightsome, full of comeliness.
The walls were freshly beaded.
Seven small birds sang entrenched in a gilded cage,
And cushions were strewn about the floor
Like colourful wedges of dimpled fat.

On the morning I walked out,
The rain was driving into my face
With a fresh, sulphurous taste.
My vision was refreshed
By the sight of flames leaping
From the peaks of nether worlds.

And then I saw her coming,
Floating towards me
Like some vision of herself
To be grasped at, fleetingly,
Before it disappeared.

I snatched her up into my arms,
Squeezing her like some childhood doll,
The one my mother bought me in the war,
And which for so long was kept in a drawer,
Limbs awkwardly disposed, greying,
Eyeless, damply cold.

The queen of it all

At last I was emboldened to ask her
What her name was, where she had come from.
She seemed disinclined to tell me.

She had that look of some vanished kingdom,
Magnificent once, and now absent,
Its great walls tumbled in ruins,

Bindweed threading its way between courses
Of masonry, strewn in the desert.
And there I was, walking, wholly bewildered,

Picking with my feet through the sands of the desert,
Imagining the triumphs of great, lost kingdoms,
Imagining her the queen of it all, yes, that benighted.

The stooped-back man

I invite you to speak on my behalf.
I listen to your words.
They are not exactly my words.

I offer you different words,
The words I might have chosen
Had I chosen to speak on my own behalf.

You dash them out of my hand
Like letters from some game of Scrabble.
Awestruck, I am quickly down on my knees

Sorting my few precious words.
They are not just anyone's words.
They are my words.

Meanwhile, you go on talking.
Little by little I become attuned
To what you are saying.

Little by little a portrait of myself
Begins to emerge -
A stooped-back man, in tears, on his knees,

Fooling with words
On some stretch of threadbare carpet.
Pity that man, I say to myself.

And pity she who has chosen to own him.

The kites

The red kite is hovering above my head,
The first in these parts for seven hundred years.
She stands with me. She too is a stranger,
The first of her kind for many long months.

She looks like a woman, but she too is a raptor.
Her teeth are well filed, the claws of her nails extended.
She circles and circles me like a kite above my kingdom.

Soon she will descend upon me.
There will be much blood, much rending,
And a heap of useless feathers.

Wholly ignoring the kite above my head,
The kite at my side,
I sidestep gingerly in the direction of
My very particular Iron Age Fort.

Reginald Hartley Eakins

Stare hard into my eyes, she said,
And see what you find there.
I looked, and found a future for myself.
The tones were warm-brown, somewhat neutral.
All seemed open-handed.

Raise up my heart, she said,
And feel what beats there.
I did as she asked.
Though slippery and furless,
It twitched in my hand like a baby rabbit.

Now open my mouth, she said,
And tell me its answers.
I plucked them out, one by one,
Deft as any top-notch orthodontist.
The first, like a child's gay streamer,
Was a long list of groceries -
From safety matches, to rum.
The second: just a hint of disquiet
About the world's weather.
And the third, a little blurry and chewed over,
Was a man's name, Reginald Hartley Eakins, my own.

Edging across linoleum

She speaks loosely to me,
Eye-beams dipped to the road,
As though conversing with a stranger.

Her hands hang in the air,
Flapping occasionally,
Like newly washed clothes in the wind.

I recognise those clothes she is wearing.
They are the same old clothes she always wore,
A good investment in their day,
Less lightsome now.

My thoughts are of a single harsh grey blanket
Hanging from the end of the bed,
Nearly touching the floor,

With its urinous puddle
Edging across linoleum
As ancient and crackled as our bold twin faces.

Flying east

May I thank you for allowing me
To be the custodian of your coat
Throughout this eleven-hour flight?
It has been my privilege, if not my honour,
To serve you throughout the night.

May I offer you seventeen small portions of food
In these delicate ceramic bowls?
Eat each one thoughtfully.
Then you may wish to doze.

You have asked me why my smile never changes.
It became attached to me
As a very small child,
And what has attached tends to remain.

May I thank you for your presence today.
It has been such a pleasure to serve.
You wish to know who I am?
Once I was a grain of seed amongst millions.
Now I am my country's representative.
Please stay with us just as long
As your visa says that you can.

A chance encounter at Peking Railway Station

When I enter the Office for the Old and Disabled,
They are all there to greet me,
Aunts, uncles, and even my ancestors.

Mr Chang enquires after the Ming bowl
From which he took his tea
In the fifteenth century.

I tell him that it is perfectly sound,
And that, on ceremonial occasions only,
We bring it out
To marvel at the fineness of its making -
How thin it is, and so perfectly round.

My great-great uncle gives me a serious bow -
Which I return, of course, with due reverence.
He tilled his fields, day in, day out,
Garnering chrysanthemums, spinach, tea,
Sufficient and more for all his needs,
Until his sad death -
Gored on the horns of his water buffalo -
In 1873.

I smile at them, routinely gathered there
In the fullness of their pride,
In the Office for the Old and Disabled
At Peking Railway Station,
All preparing now
For that great journey South,
Through the snow.

I smile and, jauntily waving, let them go.

The impatience of the emperor's new concubine

Carry me today to the Emperor's side.
I have lain here too long with all the wives.

They are all so loud and so obscene.
I am a small, young flower,
   still waiting to be seen.

One day they will come and carry me from this place
To the bed of the Emperor,
   that highest of high places.

I will be unwrapped, and presented to him
   as a prize.
He will have a child by me who will shine
   as bright

As any sun must shine because he will be
   the newest sun.
And I will lie there, basking in the warmth of him,
Proud to have done what I have done.

The woman of the Luo family

Here I wait, squatting on my haunches
at the corner of the field.

Men and women pass me by.
They do not know me.

Once I lived in the village of Cheng Kan,
a young woman, blameless.

Since my father's cousin walked in my shadow,
I have been nothing and no one.

They took me by the arm, roughly,
to the family temple.

I stared at the statues of my ancestors.
They regarded me coldly.

They pointed to the family rules
on the walls of the temple.

I read them and re-read them.
There was nothing I could do to explain.

He came behind me, a big man,
Paddling his feet, and grunting like swine.

He was hurrying in my wake.
Time was short. The light was going.

If I had met his eye, I would have said nothing.
There was nothing to be said.

I lay face down in the frozen snow,
Wondering where I began and where I ended.

I lived in the village of Cheng Kan.
I see it still, on the horizon.

No matter how many miles I walk,
I will never reach it.

I have no rice in my hand. The bowl lies in the yard,
shattered into tiny pieces.

I had a name I was born with.
And now, having lost the trust of my ancestors,
I am nothing and no one.

When the icicles hang from the eaves

When the icicles hang from the eaves,
In that month you will find me,
Still giggling at your approach,
Making light of your so-called jokes.

When the icicles hang from the eaves,
Carry one candle for me.
Place my photograph beside your flickering light.
That way it will be all right.

When the icicles hang from the eaves,
Walk with me to that house in the trees
Where we stopped and listened, so long ago,
For the silence that precedes the snow.

Snow in Tokyo

Everywhere there is an unaccustomed snow.
I do not know what to do with my feet.
I do not know what to do with my legs.
To raise them high is never high enough.
To push them forward is too much for my strength.
So I remain here, seated in the corner
        of this restaurant
Watching the cars creep through the slush...

Men are waving and shouting.
Cops are loud-hailing until their lungs
        almost burst.
I wrap my hands around my cup.
I bury myself deep inside my clothes.
My chair will be empty today.
The supervisor will be alone
        in his windowed office,
Fretting, looking out,
And damp in all his several parts.

Approaching Shanghai Pudong Airport

New forests are growing
Beside the airport road.
Where did all those peasants go
Who worked these fields in my father's time?
All, all swept aside.

Ornamental gardens are flourishing
Between the loops of the autoroute.
Who tends these gardens?
The same peasants who were plucked from the fields
Have been transplanted here.

See how they swing hard with their mattocks,
Dig deep with their spades
Until the sweat shines on their brows.
There is no word for yesterday.
All eyes are upon the future now.